the PICT
and their PLACE NAMES

W.F.H. Nicolaisen

ISBN 09515-778-6-7

Acknowledgements

Some of the initial research for material used in this essay was supported by a grant from the National Endowment for the Humanities.

Maps I and II are here reproduced with the permission of the Trustees of the Conference of Scottish Medievalists. They were first published in An Historical Atlas of Scotland c.400-c.1600, edited by Peter McNeill and Ranald Nicholson (St. Andrews 1975).

Map III is here reproduced by permission Mr Ian A. Fraser. It was first published in Alan Small (ed.), The Picts: A New Look at Old Problems (Dundee 1987).

Printed by A4 Print, Inverness.
Produced by Groam House Museum.

Introduction

The task of "translating" a lecture given orally, based on notes and aided by handouts, into a written text is never easy. Like stories, lectures are created in that space between lecturer and audience and they thrive on positive audience reaction. Delivery and reception happen simultaneously, and the encoded spoken word is immediately decoded by those who are listening. Written presentations, on the other hand, like this brief essay, are usually written in isolation, without the benefit of audience participation, and addressed to an elusive readership who lacks the guidance of voice, gesture and elaborating aside. Lectures are fleeting occasions with no expectation of any permanent validity of the views expressed or of a stylistic polish which leaves no sentence unfinished. Lectures instruct and entertain through their immediacy, opinions can be challenged and explained in the discussions which usually follow, and the captivity of the audience does not require much coaxing, teasing or winning over. In written presentations, the audience still has to be captured and is always on the point of escaping, unless shepherded with both gentleness and firmness into the desired fold. Stylistic felicity rather than mere competence are their hallmark, or at least should be, and it should be possible for readers to read sentences or whole portions over and over again without them getting the impression that the initial opacity of a statement or an argumentation hides some fraudulent manipulation of their thoughts or flawed interpretation of the patterns derived from the evidence which serves as a primary source for their distillation.

Some lecturers try to circumnavigate the shallows and submerged rocks which are strewn in the narrows that are to be crossed between oral and written form(ulation) by reading a paper which is ready for publication, footnotes and all, thus "translating" the visual to the audible, and some of them, understanding the differences between the two media, bring it off. In many instances, however, such a paper, however well it may read afterwards, fails to light the spark which is necessary to make an oral communicative act a success. The scholar who strives to achieve the opposite is not any better off, and frequently the gulf between the two media is felt to be so great that the resulting written "translation" of the oral original bears little resemblance to it so that those readers who were present at the lecture hardly recognise the written rendering they now read as being the same as the oral version they once heard.

I am extremely conscious of the pitfalls involved but will nevertheless try to give this essay a shape – in syntax, in word choice, in illustrative examples – which makes its close links with the original lecture obvious and immediately recognisable without ignoring the demands which a written text makes on any writer. This may mean that the end product will fall between the proverbial "two stools" – I hope not. My decision to follow this route, however, definitely implies that what follows in the body of this essay is not intended to be, and therefore not to be taken to be, either a comprehensive survey of all the material or a definitive interpretation of it. There will be much speculation in what I have to offer – just as there was on May 12, 1995 at Groam House when this lecture was given – but I hope that what appears to be somewhat, or even highly, speculative is not far off the mark and is imaginative as well as persuasive enough to be found acceptable, thus extending the boundaries of our knowledge of the Picts and their place names beyond the present borders of that knowledge. Perhaps it will become clear in the process that toponymic evidence, i.e. geographical names, are in spite of some of their obvious limitations, ideal raw material when it comes to an investigation of people like the Picts.

The Picts

The peculiar position in which, as the result of the current state of research into the Picts, we find ourselves forces us to consider the possibility of having to distinguish between "archaeological" Picts and "linguistic" Picts, insofar as there is no exact congruency between the distribution maps which we are able to construct on the basis of the material and artistic evidence on the one hand,[1] and the linguistic, mostly toponymic, evidence, on the other.[2] Depending on one's perspective, one can either say that the former incorporate the latter, or that the former are more extensive than the latter. There appears to be some common ground between, for example, the distribution of certain types of symbol stones and the spatial scatter of what, in this essay, we are going to term "Pictish" place names,[3] but in general we may have to admit that there is the possibility of linguistic diversity in the face of archaeological unity, unless the terminological division into Northern and Southern Picts which archaeologists tend to employ is more than a convenient geographical distinction and represents recognisable sub-divisions in Pictish material culture. If one were tempted to take an extreme – some might say, bizarre – view, one might, in fact, wonder whether the "Picts" whom the archaeologists have in mind are the same "Picts" to whom students of language and place names ascribe certain types of toponyms. This is not the view which will be taken in this essay but it would be unrealistic to ignore the fact that we are faced with a puzzling dichotomy, a convincing explanation for which has still to be found.[4]

It is, of course, self-evident that the "Picts" of this essay are defined by linguistic and onomastic criteria, whatever their material culture may have been. It also follows that only evidence, like certain place names, which can be reliably etymologised and linguistically identified can form a sound basis for this investigation, excluding therefore names for which no linguistically satisfying explanation has been found so far. Such a strategy also implies that names which have been satisfactorily ascribed to Germanic languages or to Celtic languages such as Gaelic and Cumbric have to be eliminated from our scrutiny. This is particularly necessary with regard to Gaelic which belongs to a different branch of Celtic and to Cumbric which was spoken south of what one might call the "Pictish" heartland, in terms of our toponymic criteria. If, then, the language of the Picts was identical neither with Gaelic[6] nor with Cumbric[7] and certainly not with Germanic,[8] what are the possibilities which offer themselves? (A) "Pictish" may have been a Celtic language other than the two subdivisions already mentioned, and it may at one time have been spoken throughout the area ascribed to the "Picts" by students of material culture but may later have been "lost" in one part of it while continuing to exist in another until at least the ninth century when it was replaced by Gaelic.[9] (B) There were two "Pictish" languages, one Celtic and the other of unknown origin and ascription but definitely not Indo-European; these two languages were spoken in different parts of the area associated by the archaeologists with the "Picts".[10] (C) "Pictish" was a non-Celtic, non Indo-European language at one time spoken throughout archaeological "Pictland".[11] A recent study, for example, claims that the Pictish inscriptions show it to have been distantly related to the Caucasian languages,[12] and similar, astonishing theories have been advanced from time to time over the years.

For the purposes of our current exploration, which will be limited to the study of toponymic evidence linked with the Picts, option (C) will not be considered since the place names in question are clearly Celtic. As these geographical names are found in a restricted area, their absence from other parts of Scotland in which "Pictish" material remains have been discovered has, within the context of this examination, to remain a question without a satisfactory answer. The presence, in what might at one time have been "Greater Pictland", of major island names such as Unst, Yell, Fetlar, Lewis, Uist, Skye, Islay, Arran which, in spite of secondary reinterpretations in terms of later languages, cannot be convincingly associated with any linguistic points of reference; of what look like Indo-European but not Celtic river names, like Shin, Shiel, Farrar, Findhorn, Deveron, Earn, and Tay; and of the odd "difficult" river name, like the Spey, can only be taken into account on the periphery of this essay, although they certainly cannot be ignored.

The 'Picts' who are thought to be responsible for the corpus of geographical names which forms the substance of this discussion[14] are not mentioned by name until the end of the third century A.D., and the first reference to the meaning of their name is recorded at the end of the fourth century when the classical writer Claudian refers to them as *noc falso nomine Pictos* "the well-named Picts" thus perpetuating what is likely to have been a Roman soldiers' folk-etymology, deriving the name from, or at least equating it with, the Latin adjective *pictus* "painted, tattooed".

'Whether this derivation also led to the belief that the Picts painted or tattooed themselves or whether they actually did so and therefore reinforced the Romans' linguistic perception, is another interesting question which does, however, not concern us here as the link with Latin *pictus* is at best a secondary reinterpretation in the medium of another language. We have no evidence what the Picts called themselves but the exonyms which their neighbours had for them confirm that the name underlying Latin *Picti* was certainly the name by which other people knew and referred to them. In Old Norse they are called *Pettar* or *Pettir* (Historia Norvegicae: *Peti*), and in the Anglo-Saxon Chronicle they appear as *Pehtas, Pihtas, Pyhtas, Peohtas* and *Piohtas*, and there are related Anglian personal names on record such as *Peohthelm, Peohtred, Peohtwealt, Peohtwine*, and *Peohtwulf*). In Old Scots they are known as *Pecht*, and the Welsh called them *Peith-wyr*. The name is also contained in the name Pentland Firth (Old Norse *Petlandsfjorðr*; Latin *Petlandicum Mare*) and possibly in that of the *Pentland Hills*, potentially, and very roughly, the northern and southern boundaries of 'Pictland', i.e. the Picts were understood to live to the south of the one and for the north of the other.[15] The latter perception is reinforced by the Ravenna Geographer's *Pexa* which, though listed as the name of a fort on the Antonine Wall, may, according to Rivet and Smith, stand "for *Pecti* or, even more interestingly, **Pectia* 'Pictland'", perhaps with an intermediate form **Pext(i)a*.[16] Although the Cosmographer's work was not compiled until the beginning of the eighth century A.D. it is thought that its source for Northern Britain was a Severan modernisation (208-211 A.D.) of an official military map of Flavian times (69-96 A.D.). Since the information this contained was mostly gathered during Agricola's campaigns (77-83 A.D.), this would, if this hypothesis is sustainable, make *Pexa* (<**Pectia*) the earliest reference for the Picts and Pictland.

If the Roman etymology were correct, *Pict-*, or rather *Pect-*, would go back to an Indo-European root **peik-* 'painted' but if that were so, the Celtic derivative would have lost its initial *p-*, thus leaving us with something like •ekt-. A *p*-Celtic *Pict* (<*Pekt-) is, however, to be expected to have started out as something like **Quekt-*, whatever that may have meant, and a meaning like 'painted' is unacceptable. The most closely related names are *Poitiers* and *Poitou* in France, which started out as *Pictones* and *Pictavi*, respectively, but it would be highly speculative to connect the Gaulish tribes with our Picts, on the evidence of these names alone.[17] The earliest classical writers who otherwise tend to have the most reliable information about Scotland in Roman times – Tacitus, Lucan, Martial, Ptolemy, and Cassius Dio, for instance – use the terms *Caledonii* for the tribe and *Caledonia* for their territory although it is, of course, difficult to say whether *Caledonia* is really congruent with 'Pictland', and not just one part of it.

Chronologically we therefore have to think of the "historical" Picts as having held sway from the third – or, if the interpretation of the Ravenna Geographer's *Pexa* is persuasive enough, the late first-century A.D. to the ninth century, or possibly a little longer. For that reason, it is only to be expected that, over a spread of six or even eight hundred years, a number of linguistic changes occurred, some of which are also reflected in the toponymy of Pictland. As will become evident from the corpus of place names to be discussed in the following, such changes are particularly noticeable in the morphological aspects of the names in question, i.e. a replacement of derivation, mostly through the addition of suffixes, by the compounding of two free morphemes, one of them serving as a generic, the other as a specific. Neither the language of the Picts nor the place-nomenclature created by that language may therefore be seen as static; otherwise it would be difficult, if indeed permissible, to link the earliest Pictish river names with the late Pictish place names in a Gaelicised environment. Nevertheless, for the purposes of this essay, the term Picts is uniformly used for the people, and the adjective Pictish for the language they spoke, i.e. a form of *p*-Celtic.[18]

Pictish Place Names

On the basis of a number of criteria, mostly linguistic and distributional, it is possible to isolate several Pictish place-name elements and consequently a variety of Pictish place names which contain such elements, especially as generics. Probably the best known and also most intensively studied of these is the element *Pit-*, as in *Pittenweem, Pittodrie, Pitcaple, Pitliver, Pitlochry*, and so on.[19] There appear to be over three hundred examples of this name type in Scotland, although quite a few of these are now "lost" and cannot be located anymore with any degree of precision. The main reason for ascribing this toponymic generic to a p-Celtic language and not to Gaelic is the initial *p-* sound, also to be found in such names as *Perth* or *Pressmannan*. There can be little doubt as to the meaning of this component which is generally taken to be "portion, share, piece of land". Earlier spellings of the names in which it is to be found show it to have been *pet* or *pett* in pre-medieval and medieval times, and it is thus cognate with Welsh and Cornish *peth* "thing" and Breton *pez* "piece", all deriving from an earlier *petia* in which form it was adopted by the Latin of Roman Gaul and, as a French loan-word, subsequently gave us English *piece*.

Pett is first mentioned in the 12th-century Aberdeenshire *Book of Deer* in which reference is made to *Pett in Mulenn* "portion of the Mill", *Pett Malduibh* "Malduibh's portion", *Pett meic Garnait* "Garnat's son's portion" and *Pett meic Cobroig* "Cobroch's son's portion".[20] It is unlikely that these four instances are purely lexical but rather represent named places although these cannot now be identified. What is, however, significant is that all the specifics, including the three personal names, are Gaelic, not Pictish, and that their grammar is also Gaelic. This is, in fact, symptomatic of the great majority of *Pit-* names and, while part translations are a possibility, it has to be assumed that the Pictish term *pet(t)* was adopted by the Gaelic-speaking incomers of Pictland, both lexically and onomastically, and was then used in the formation of Gaelic place names in the area. Only a small number of Pit- names contain specifics that can definitely be said to be Pictish; among these are *Pitpointie* in Angus (*Petponti[n]* 13th century) "bridge portion", *Pitbladdo* in Fife "flour portion", and *Pitfour* in Perthshire (*Pitfur* 1357) "pasture portion", but even *Pitbladdo* shows early, though perhaps only temporary, Gaelicisation (*Petblatho* 1481), and *Pitfour* may have the Gaelic loan-word *pór* as a specific, rather than the Pictish original. The conclusion is inevitable that most of the *Pit-* names were coined by speakers of Gaelic and not by speakers of Pictish; they therefore lay themselves open to the criticism that, because of their "hybrid" nature, they are of little value as evidence for a Pictish presence and that consequently their geographical distribution is suspect when it is interpreted as indicative of the settlement area of the Celtic-speaking Picts. Fortunately, it is possible to counter this argument which at first glance seems to have some justification by pointing out that the limited scatter of the three hundred or so Scottish place names which can be said to contain this element (Map 1) are an indication that the term, and the concomitant notion of, Pictish *pett* was, on the whole, adopted and used only in what had previously been "Pictland", and that at least its toponymic usage had in post-Pictish times not spread beyond that area, with the exception of perhaps a handful of examples. It is therefore the general contention of

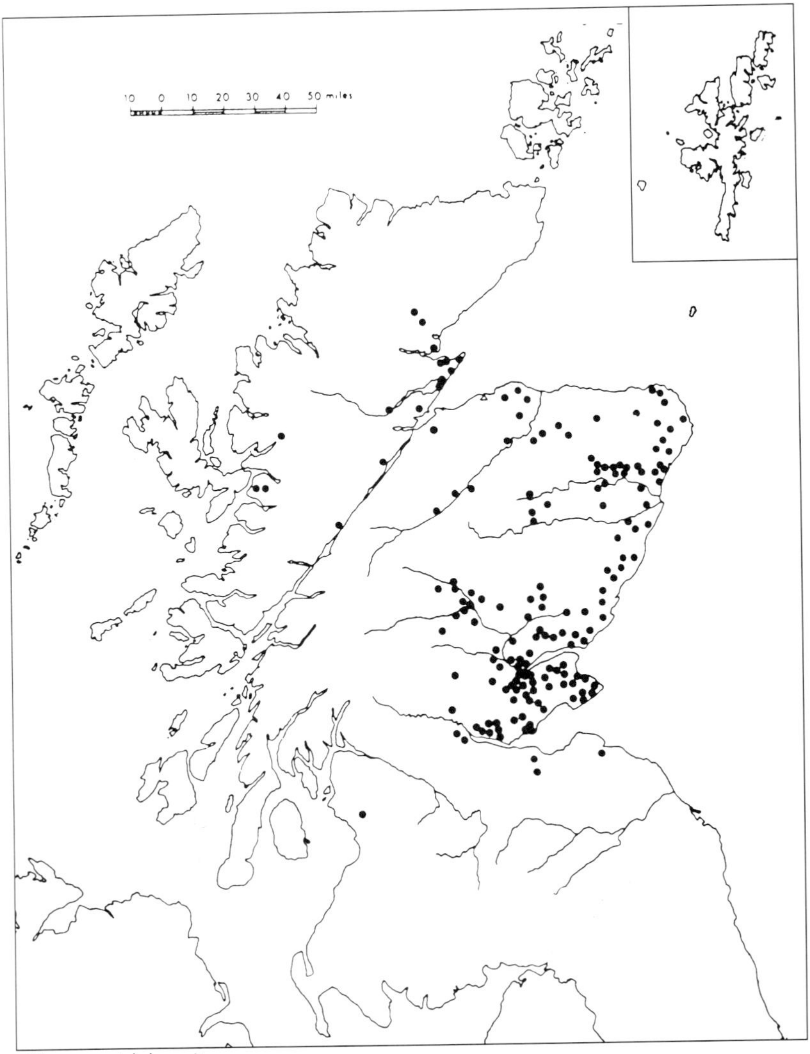

• Name containing *pit*

MAP I

name scholars that *all* the *Pit-* names, including the many which contain Gaelic specifics, are valid evidence for a visual representation of what once was the settlement area of the Celtic-speaking Picts.

It follows from these observations that *Pit-* names in which *pet(t)* serves as a generic are, from a chronological point of view, rather late newcomers on the Pictish scene, many of them being post-Pictish, and one might even be led to the conclusion that their heyday was after the Pictish era had effectively come to an end. The fact that, apart from a few exceptions, all the *Pit-* names are compound names is morphological confirmation of their relative lateness. As place names do not normally wear the dates of their creation on their sleeves it is, of course, impossible to say when *pet(t)* first became productive as a Pictish place-name component but its presence in Romano-Gaulish is a hint that its usage may have been latent throughout Pictish times while the actualisation of such potential usage may well have taken place not before, let us say, the seventh or eighth century; its post-Pictish productivity may, on the other hand, have lasted into the tenth century or, in certain instances, even longer.

As Map 1 demonstrates, *Pit-* names are to be found from the Firth of Forth northwards as far as the Moray Firth and, with less density, in Easter Ross and south-east Sutherland, the Dornoch Firth appearing to have been an effective northern boundary.[21] In the west, some names occur in western Perthshire and in Badenoch but in general they are not to be found west of the Great Glen. The few stragglers south of the Firth of Forth are exceptions which prove the rule rather than contradict it; otherwise the distribution of *Pit-* names in Scotland is compact and well-defined and deserves the epithet "Pictish". It also coincides roughly with what classical and other sources described or referred to as Pictish territory.

It is their remarkably neat and tidy geographical distribution which conclusively links them with the Picts, and ultimately the Picts alone, that has made *Pit-* names the darlings of toponymic research in Pictland and which has claimed the attention of scholars working in ancillary disciplines, principally geographers. First and foremost among the geographical investigations of *Pit-* name sites are the studies of Whittington and Soulsby, with the aim of gathering information about "the preferred habitat of the Pictish people".[22] Investigating the *Pit-* name sites of Fife and the adjacent parts of Angus in considerable detail, they come to the conclusion that the Picts generally did not favour the coastal zone and also avoided the floors of river valleys and that, because of the largely coastal area below and the adverse exposure conditions above, *Pit-* names are almost entirely distributed between an altitude of 50 and 650 feet. Altitude is, however, not the only factor which influenced the dwellers on *Pit-* name sites in their preferred choices; other considerations, sometimes linked to altitude, also come into play. The distance from one *Pit-* name to another varies from between ¼ and 3½ miles but the settlement pattern has to be understood as clustered rather than random. Loamy soils, often developed from the till of the volcanic rocks, as well as calciferous sandstone, where till-covered, proved particularly attractive to the Picts, especially when the chosen sites also provided shelter and good drainage. A southerly component in the aspect of the site and protection from the direction of the prevailing winds were also significant factors in the choice of sites which tended to be located on the sides of eminences which rose steeply behind the site while providing a gentle slope in front which would facilitate the natural drainage of the soil. The fact that there are more than a dozen examples of the name *Pittendreich* (with variants) "portion of the aspect" is toponymic confirmation of Whittington's and Soulsby's findings, and one might regard these names as the Pictish equivalents of modern names like *Blinkbonny*, *Morningside* or *Sunnybank*. Undoubtedly, the farmers among the Picts chose the best sites available. In their day they may have had an almost completely free choice when looking for such sites although they did, of course, have to compete with other similarly-minded Picts.

Recently, Simon Taylor, in his Edinburgh Ph.D. thesis on *Settlement names in Fife*, suggested that in Fife *pett* did became an appellative in Gaelic and not just a toponymic element, as Jackson had thought, and that as such it was used an an active place-name element for at least 200 years, from the middle of the ninth to the middle of the eleventh century.[24] While accepting the usually advanced etymology of *pett* and its basic meaning as "portion", he thinks that it was particularly and more specifically used to refer to a dependent estate within the shire. According to Taylor, these dependent estates called *pett* no doubt also had some fiscal and administrative meaning, now lost, within the Pictish kingdom and he believes that this meaning continued right up until the introduction of the feudal system in the twelfth century.[25] This is a persuasive argument but one cannot help wondering whether all the 78 *Pit-* names in Fife, 18 of which are now "lost", would fit that particular meaning, perhaps a more cautious approach would suggest that while some of the sites to which *Pit-*

names were given achieved that status, not all of them did. It is also still open to question whether the conclusions reached by Whittington and Soulsby on the one hand and Taylor on the other, are applicable beyond Fife and southern Angus. A comprehensive and systematic examination of all Pit- name sites wherever they occur is therefore still a strong desideratum. Nevertheless, the results of both geographical and historical research into the *Pit-* names in Fife are an encouraging indication of how much more this kind of place-name evidence has to offer when properly and imaginatively interrogated.

Another approach, more onomastically oriented, is a close scrutiny of the specifics which are attached to *pet(t)* in those names for which we can establish, with a reasonable degree of certainty, their lexical meaning. Certain major categories emerge with ease:

Personal Names

Pitkerrald INV 'St. Cyril's portion'
Petultin (1144) FIF 'Ultan's portion'
Pethergus (1195) KCD 'Fergus's portion'
Pitmaduthie ROS 'Macduff's portion'
Petmacduffgyl (14c?) PER 'portion of Dugald's sons'
Pitcarmick PER 'Cormac's portion'
Pitkennedy ANG 'Cenneteigh's portion'
Pitmurchie ABD 'Murchadh's portion'
Pitcaithlie PER 'Cathalan's portion'
Pitmiclardie FIF 'MacLaverty's portion'
Pitelpie ANG 'Alpin's portion'
Pitewan ANG 'Eughan's portion'
Pitkenny FIF 'Kenneth's portion'
Pitcalman INV 'Calman's portion'
Pitconnequhy ROS 'Duncan's portion'

Occupations, etc.

Pitlour KNR 'Leper's portion'
Pettinseir MOR 'Craftsman's portion'
Pittentagart ABD 'Priest's portion'
Pithogarty ROS 'Priest's portion'
Pittagarty (1598) MOR 'Priest's portion'
Pettincleroch (1489) PER 'Portion of the Clerics'

Institutions, etc.
Pittenhaglis (1511) FIF 'Church's portion'
Pettintoscale (1450) STL 'the Gospel's portion'
Pettintoscall (1410) ANG 'the Gospel's portion'
Pettuscal (1590) FIF 'the Gospel's portion'
Pitliver FIF 'Portion of the Book, i.e. the Bible'
Pitcastle PER 'Castle portion'
Pitmillan ABD 'Portion of the Mill'
Petmolin FIF 'Portion of the Mill'
Pett in Mulenn ABD 'Portion of the Mill'
Petcurren alias *Petbrain* (1564) PER 'Queen portion'

Agriculture
Pitarrow FIF, ANG 'corn share'
Pitbladdo FIF 'flour share'

Pastoral
Pitfour SUT, etc. 'Pasture portion'
Pitcaple ABD 'Horse portion'
Pitgaveny ABD 'Stirk portion'
Pettymuck ABD 'Pig portion'
Pittenfarrow ABD 'Bull portion'
Pittendamph ABD 'Ox portion'
Pitgoberis (1593) PER 'Goat portion'
Petmarch (1526) FIF 'Horse portion'
Pettyvaich INV, BNF 'Byre portion'

Measurements
Pitcog PER 'Portion of the fifth part'
Pitcox ELD 'Portion of the fifth part'
Pitkerrow ANG 'Portion of the fourth part'

Surroundings
Pitpointie ANG 'Bridge portion'
Pitcorthie FIF 'Pillar-stone portion'
Pitforthie KCD, ANG 'Pillar-stone portion'
Pitlochry PER 'Stony portion' (Stepping stones)
Pitlochrie ANG 'Stony portion' (Stepping stones)
Pitmurthly PER 'Portion of the Big Hill'
Pittenweem FIF 'Portion of the Cave'

Pittencrieff FIF 'Tree portion'
Pitcruvie FIF 'Tree portion (?)'
Pitcruive PER 'Tree portion (?)'
Pitchirn INV 'Rowan Tree portion'
Pitcowden ABD 'Hazel portion'
Pitcows KCD 'Holly portion'
Pitcullen ABD, PER 'Holly portion'
Pitfoules (1698) FIF 'Stream portion'
Pittilloch FIF 'Hill portion'
Petmaurcha (1628) FIF 'Portion of the Cast' (Urquhart)

Situation
Pitmedden ABD 'middle portion'
Pitmain INV 'middle portion'
Pittendreich, etc. 'aspect portion'

Others
Pitlurg BNF, ABD 'portion of the shank'
Pitsligo ABD 'shelly portion'
Pitcroy MOR 'hard portion'
Pitfoskie ABD 'shelter portion'
Pitarrick PER 'portion of the pulling' (brae)
Pitglassie ROS 'lea portion'

This is, of course, only a small portion of the total number of *Pit-* names but the names concerned nevertheless give us some insight into the everyday life and world-view of those who named these sites and lived in them. For example, personal ownership of the topographical feature termed *pet(t)* is clearly possible; in many instances the actual name of an owner is recorded; for example, in the glosses from the *Book of Deer* all the proprietors, or persons in some way associated with the *pet(t)*, have Gaelic names. The church emerges as a major proprietor, sometimes represented by the priest, often through symbolic, presumably dedicatory reference. Several "portions" belong to the mill or miller; at least one is associated with a castle nearby. Several *Pit-* names record pastoral activities, specifying the animal to be pastured as horse, pig, goat, stirk, ox and bull. The reference to a byre, or perhaps cattle enclosure, implies the keeping of cows. Land division or measurement into quarters or five parts is indicated by some names, and frequently a *pet(t)* is identified by a prominent feature nearby, whether natural (hill, cave, tree, rowan, hazel, holly or stream) or manmade (bridge, pillar stone, stepping stones). The situation of the *pet(t)*, its shape or condition also are used as identifying devices. The three major differentiating factors are therefore ownership, utilisation, and visual cross-reference to a neighbouring landscape feature. Agricultural activities, with a special emphasis on their pastoral aspects, point to the nature of *pet(t)s* as farm, sometimes perhaps with specialised purposes. As already indicated above, many names of the *Pittendreich* type express the pleasant or desirable location of the named "portion", possibly with a certain amount of pride by the owner. These names may well make implied reference to a particularly attractive view, too, thus anticipating many a modern house name like Hillview, Bayview, Ochilview, Viewforth and the like. Quite clearly, inhabitants of *pet(t)s* did not work all the time but allowed themselves some time to sit back and relax and admire the view. The clustering of *pet(t)s* is possibly implied by names like *Petty* INV, Garlic *Peitigh*, the dative or locative of *peiteach* 'place of *petts*'.

How important it is to search for an pay attention to early spellings is demonstrated by the Aberdeenshire name *Pitfodels* which is *Badfothel* in 1157, a form which exposes it as a false *Pit-* name, while at the same time bearing witness to *pet(t)* as a dominant or at least common place-name element at the time when the change took place, probably in the fifteenth century (*Petfodellis* 1488). The replacement of a similarly sounding element like Gaelic *bad* "a clump' by *pet-* is, however, a much less frequent occurrence than the substitution of Gaelic *baile* for *pet*, at least in the Gaelic variant of the name in question. This has happened in[27]

Pitfour SUT = Gaelic *Baile-phùir*
Pitkerrie ROS = Gaelic *Baile-céirigh*
Pitlochry PER = Gaelic *Baile a' Chlaichrigh*
Pitcastle PER = Gaelic *Baile a'Chaisteil*
Pitarrick PER = Garlic *Baile an Tarraig*
Pitglassie R OS = Gaelic *Baile a'Ghlasaich*
Pitmaduthie ROS = Gaelic *Baile mhic Dhuibh*
or *Pit mhic Dhuibh*

All the names just quoted are found in areas in which Gaelic was spoken until recently or is still spoken today, and the reason of the substitution of *baile* for *pet(t)* seems to be that the Gaelic form of the latter, *peit*, has colloquially potential obscene connotations through reference to the female genitals. As Simon Taylor points out, however, this cannot have been the reason in medieval Fife from which he quotes the 1623 entry *Pittullye 'alias' Batullye* in the *Register of the Great Seal* for the name *Baltilly*, as well as similar substitutions in such names as *Balgeddie, Bantuscall* and *Garriech*. He explains the Fife substitutions as having their origin in references to different aspects of the same feature so that "*pett* may well have referred to the full estate with whatever tenurial obligations went with it, while *baile* was part of that estate, perhaps the arable core, or even the chief place of habitation".[28] These two meanings may have got blurred when *baile* became the dominant toponymic element referring to a human habitation. Substitutions of any kind, however interesting in themselves, are, however, very much the exception rather than the rule. The fact that they occur so rarely, even in bilingual situations, emphasises the inherent stability of *pet(t)* > *pit* as a place-name element, even in a new linguistic environment.

Pet(t) is by far the most common toponymic generic which we can safely associate with the Picts. It is without a doubt its numerical strength as well as its geographical distribution which has made it such a favourite among students of Pictish toponymy. For this reason it has almost become an onomastic symbol of "Pictishness" in spite of its late flowering and its extended productivity in post-Pictish Gaelic times. Scholarly preoccupation with Pit- names has, however, also had its risks, not only because other elements have been neglected but especially because this neglect has deprived us of a more rounded picture of what the Pictish toponymic heritage stands for. None of the other toponymic generics and name types which can be ascribed to Pictish has the same territorial exclusiveness as *pet(t)*; they all lack therefore the impressive, almost dramatic, quality of being only Pictish and nothing else. Chief among these other elements is the generic *aber* "confluence, river mouth" which in its Scottish distribution is mainly to be found in the same area as *pet(t)* but which also occurs in Cumbric territory south of the Forth-Clyde line (*Abercarf, Aberlosk, Abermilk*) and also, of course, in Wales (*Abergavenny, Aberystwyth, Aberdare*, etc.).[29] In contrast to *pet(t)*, it therefore removes Pictish from its isolation and links it with other *p*-Celtic (Brythonic, Brittonic) languages, thus correcting the somewhat lopsided image of Pictish as a separate linguistic entity. (Map II) This does not mean, of course, that *aber* is not legitimately Pictish in the linguistic Pictland mapped out by *pet(t)* – quite the contrary; it only lacks its astonishing restriction to this Pictland as defined by *pet(t)*. Secondly it is

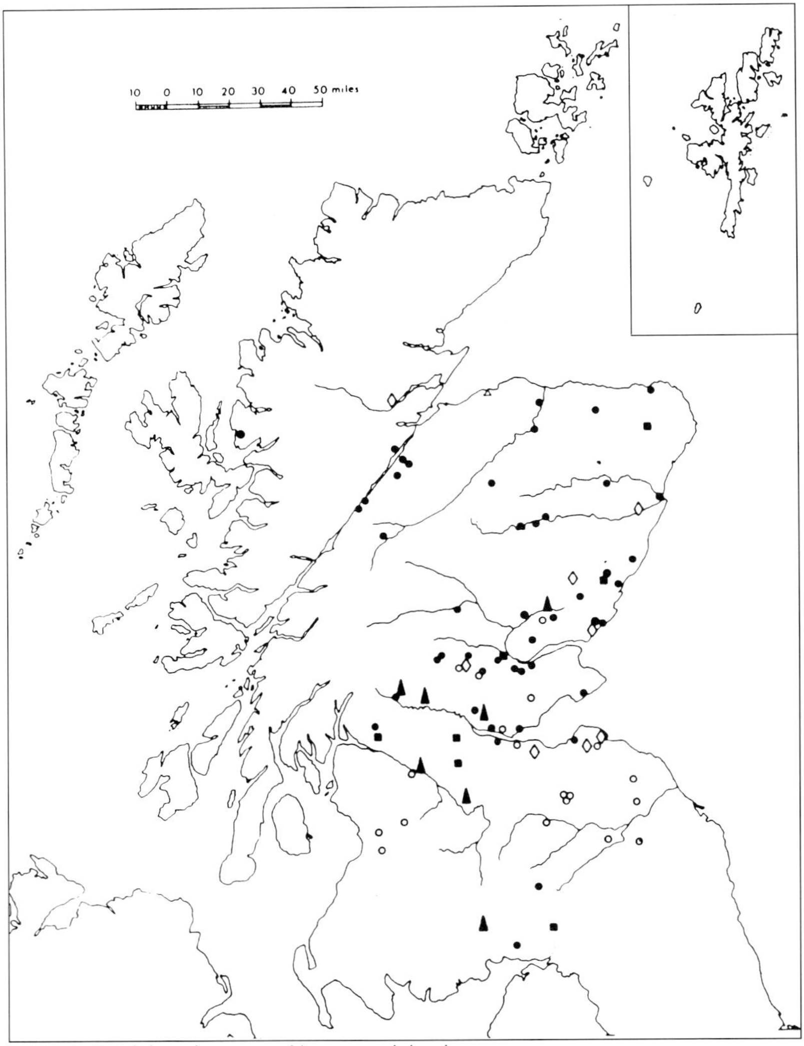

● Name containing *aber*
○ Name containing *pren*
■ Name containing *pert*
▲ Name containing *lanerc*
◇ Name containing *pevr*

MAP II

the location of *Aber-* names within Pictland which saves us from assuming that all Picts shunned the coastal areas and the river valleys like the farmers of the *Pit-* name sites. It goes without saying that *Aber-* names are always associated with water courses, especially their confluences, and do therefore not regularly occur at an altitude of between 50 and 650 feet like the *Pit-* names. In this respect, *Aber-* name sites complement *Pit-* name sites, and lead us to Picts whose habitat and occupations were river-related. Like their agrarian counterparts and their relationship to the most desirable locations for agricultural and pastoral activities, the ripuarian Picts must have exploited their situations on the banks of water courses and in river valleys to the full, whether for the purposes of fishing or transportation by boat, or the utilisation of the fertile alluvial soil. From such a very practical perspective river-mouths and confluences must have offered special opportunities, especially from the point of view of communication; this aspect must therefore be at least partially responsible for the creation and preservation of so many *Aber-* names by the Picts. Unlike *(pet(t)*, *aber* appears not to have been absorbed into the topononymic vocabulary of Gaelic which already had its own equivalent *Inver-* (*inbhear, inbhir*). In one known instance, *aber* was replaced by *inver- Haberberui* 1290, now *Inverbervie* KCD – and there is no reason why this should not have happened in other cases for which we lack the necessary documentary evidence. Names like *Inverpeffer* ANG and *Inverpeffray* PER come to mind which contain Pictish river names as specifics.

In the first place, then, *Aber-* names draw our attention to the fact that there were Picts who made a living from rivers and therefore regarded the vicinity of water courses as preferred habitats or settlement sites. This does not mean that there was a clear cut distinction between land-Picts and river-Picts, and we can safely assume that those Picts who lived in *petts* were aware of the *aber-* sites, and that those who had their dwellings near *abers* had at least heard of certain *Pit-* names although social intercourse between them was maybe largely restricted to commercial transactions. *Aber-* names do, however, also lead us to another corpus of Pictish geographical names, i.e. the names of water-courses. It is reasonable to think of the river names which are incorporated in *Aber-* names as having either already existed when the toponymic *aber* designation was created or, at the very latest, to have been created simultaneously with the *Aber-* name, perhaps, initially in reference to the stretch of the river near its mouth, whether on the coast or at the confluence with another, larger river.

It is not necessary to posit that the Pictish hydronymy predated the Pictish toponymy closely associated with it, although in several instances that may well have been the case. Whatever the genesis may be with regard to each individual *Aber-* name, the Picts must have known the names of the water courses in the vicinity of which the *Aber-* names are to be found, and this knowledge is not likely to have been restricted to the dwellers at those sites. In addition to place names found with the elements *pet(t)* and *aber*, we therefore have a substantial corpus of Pictish river names although many of these are difficult to trace back beyond their subsequent Gaelic and English forms.

River names belonging to this category are:

* BERBA, in Aberbervie, now Inverbervie KCD (Haberberui 1290); River Bervie, cf. Irish berbaim 'I boil'. Welsh berwi – "the boiling one".

* BODERIA, in Aberbothrie PER (Abbyrbothry, etc. 1375); tributary of the Isla, identical with Ptolemy's name for the Forth, cf. Gaelic boidhre 'deafness' – "deaf one, noiseless one".

* BRUTACA,-OS, in Arbroath ANG, Gaelic Obar-brothaig (Aberbrudoc 1189-98, Abirbrothoc 1199); Brothock Burn, cf. Gaelic bruth 'heat', and Welsh -awc, now -og, which in Gaelic has become -ág – "little boiling one". Compare also Burn of Brown BNF, Gaelic Allt Bruthain(n), from * BRUTONA.

BUADHNAT (Gaelic), in Arbuthnott KCD (Aberbothenoth 1242); tributary of Bervie, cf. Gaelic buadh 'virtue', with the diminutive suffix -n-ant- added – "little one of virtue, i.e. healing".

* CAT-, in Abercattie ABD (Abircawte 1473); South Cattie Burn; the upper reaches are called Glencat. The settlement name has been replaced by Whitehouse. Meaning unclear.

* CRUMB-, in (1) Abercrombie FIF (Abercrumbin 1153-66), and (2) Abercrombie FIF (Abercrumbin 1227); Gaelic Aberchrombaidth; cf. Welsh crwm, Gaelic crom, Old Irish cromb 'bent' – "the bent one".

* DELG-, in Aberdalgie PER (Aberdalgin 1215-21); tributary of Earn, cf. Cornish delc 'necklace', Gaelic dealg, Old Irish delg 'thorny pin' – "pin-shaped one".

* DEVONA, Aberdeen ABD, Gaelic Obar-dheathan (Aberdon 1150); River Don (Devana c. 150 AD Ptolemy), from devos 'god', cf. River Dee (Deva) – "goddess".

* DUBRON and derivatives, in Aberdour ABD (Aberdouer 1178-99) and Aberdour FIF (Abirdouer 1329); Dour Burn, cf. Welsh dwfr, dwr, Gaelic dobhar 'water' – "(flowing) water". Aberarder ABD

(Abirardoure 1451); Feardar Burn. Aberarder INV (Twa Aberardoris 1458); tributary of River Nairn. Aberarder INV (Oberarder 1696); tributary of Loch Laggan – "high water". * CALETO-DUBRON, in Aberchalder INV (Abbircaledour 1238). Gaelic Obar-Chaladair; Calder Burn – "hard water". CIAR-DOBHAR, in Aberchirder BNF (Abirkerdour c.1204); tributary of River Deveron – "black water".

* GELIDIOS/-A, in Abergeldie ABD (Aberyedly 1438), Gaelic Obar-Gheallaidh; Geldie, cf. Old Irish gel 'white', also Irish and Welsh glan 'pure' – "the white or pure one".
* LABARA, -OS, in Aberlour BNF (Abyrlouer 1224-42); Burn of Aberlour, cf. Gaelic labhar, Welsh llafar 'loud' – "the loud one".
* LEMONACA, in Aberlemno ANG (Aberlimenach 1242, Aberlevinach 1250); Lemno Burn, cf. Gaelic Lemnach, adjective from leam(h)ain, Irish lem 'elm tree' – "elm river".

LIDNAIG (Gaelic), in Aberlednock PER (Abbirlednoch 1444), Gaelic Obar-Lidnaig; Lednock Burn. Obscure.

LUATHNAT (Gaelic), in Aberluthnot KCD (Aberluthenoth 1242); tributary of North Esk, cf. Irish luath 'fast' + -n-ant- – "little swift one".

* NECTONA, in Abernethy INV (Abyrnythy 1187-1203), Gaelic Obar-neithich; River Nethy; and Abernethy PER (Aburnethiga 10c); tributary of Earn, Pictish * Neithon > Gaelic * Nethech – "pure one".

-NYTE, in Abernyte PER (Abernyde 1296); Abernyte Burn – Obscure.

* TARVOS, in Abertarff INV (Abirtarf 1208-15), Gaelic Obar-thairbh; River Tarff, cf. Welsh tarw, Gaelic tarbh 'bull' – "bull river".
* TURTHAID (Gaelic), in Aberturret PER (no early forms); Turret Burn, cf. Gaelic tur 'dry' + -that – "little dry one".
* VERGO, in Aberargie PER (Apurfeirt) [= feire] 10th cent.); twa tounis of Aberargyis 1492); River Farg, also Glenfarg, cf. Old Welsh *guerg* 'effective', Gaelic *fearg*, gen. *fairge* 'wrath' – "effective or wrathful one".

It can be taken for granted that not every Pictish river-name triggered an *Aber-* name and also that some of the *Aber-* names may now be lost, without any documentation recording their earlier existence. For these reasons, the actual inventory of Pictish names of water courses can be supposed to have been greater. We might therefore be permitted to add such names as *Abona* (Water of Aven ABD/KCD), *Bremava* (Braan PER), *Brivara* (Bruar PER), *Brutona* (Burn of Brown BNF, see under * *Brutaca* above), *Caleto-dubron* (Calder PER, Callander PER, Callater ABD, ANG, etc.), *Catona* (Inverhadden Burn PER), *Iektona* (Ythan ABD), *Isca* (Esk ANG, KCD), *Lemona* (Leven FIF), *Limenti* (Livet BNF), and *Limona* (Lyon PER). To this list one might add some major river names in Pictland which, though apparently pre-Pictish in origin, must have been known to and used by the Picts. Names in this category are the *(Find)horn*, the *(Dev)eron*, the *Nairn*, the *Earn*, the *Spey*, and probably also the *Tay*.[31]

On the other hand, there are also some *Aber-* names which do not incorporate river names but are compounded with some other specific. One of the best known of these is probably *Aberfoyle* PER (Gaelic *Obar-phuill*) which is the "mouth of the *poll* (or sluggish stream)" which even in Pictish times appears to have been unnamed. Then there is *Aberfeldie* PER (Gaelic *Obar-pheallaidh*), the "confluence of *Peallaidh*, an old water demon". *Abercairney* PER and *Abergairn* ABD are both thoroughly Pictish since their specific is *carden* "a copse", as in *Kincardine* (see below). *Abercorn* WLO (*Aebbercurnig* c.720) is the "horned confluence", presumably because of its shape; the obsolete *Aberdolo* FIF (*Aberdolloche* 1630) contains *dolach*, the old genitive of *dol* "meadow", *dol* itself being a Pictish loanword in Gaelic; *Aberlady* ELO (*Aberleuedi* 1214-29) is etymologically related to Gaelic *lobh* "putrify"; the second element in *Aber(r)uchill* PER (*Abbirruchil* 1461, *Aberurquill* 1594) is probably the phrase "on wood"; and the specific in *Aber(r)uthven* PER (*Aberruadeuien* c. 1198, *Aberrotheuin* c. 1211) implies a "red place" nearby. It is impossible to say whether some of these *Aber-* names originally contained a river name which has been replaced by another non-hydronymic element (for instance, *Aberlady* < * *Aberpeffer*) but there is no need to envision such a replacement. As is the case with so many of the river names listed above, the specific in the names just cited have undergone Gaelicisation as well as Anglicisation, and it is therefore not always easy to retrieve the original Pictish form. It is, however, more than likely that all the specifics in question started out in a Pictish-speaking environment. Some of them still bear witness to such origins. Watson specifically comments on the transition from Pictish (British) into Gaelic in connection with such names as *Aberbothrie, Abergeldie, Aberlemno* and *Abertarff.* In the last of these, the identity of Gaelic *tarbh* and *Welsh tarw* "bull" obviously facilitated the transition since only minimal phonological adjustment was required.

The identity of Pictish *aber* and Welsh *aber* has sometimes been questioned or even denied, especially by those who are convinced that Pictish is a Goidelic, not a Brittonic language. One of the chief arguments thrown into the debate by adherents of that theory is the observation that several of the *Aber-* name sites are not located at the very mouth or confluence which they are supposed to designate, and a Gaelic term *eabar* "marsh" has therefore been proposed as the more likely generic.[32] This argument ignores both the fact that hardly ever do local conditions allow settlements to be built close to the mouth of a water course, and the frequent transfer of a topographical name to a nearby village or farm for which there are numerous examples involving other topographic generics. Such transfers may well have included an intermediate stage when the topographical feature and the human settlement nearby shared the same name although it was separately applied. Such a double existence is still very common elsewhere, regardless of whether the naming of the natural feature preceded the naming of the human habitation or occurred simultaneously with the latter. Whatever the situation may have been in the cases of individual *Aber-* names, it is unhelpful to continue to doubt the close connection between Pictish and Welsh *aber* by denying that Pictish *aber* designates a "confluence" or "river-mouth".

Having made this point as strongly as one can possibly make it, one must nevertheless concede that this basic and repeated meaning may not have been the *only* meaning of *aber* in a number of instances in Pictland. Taking the name *Aberdeen* "Don-mouth" as our starting point, we cannot help noticing that, if the lexical meaning of the river name *Don* (< *Devana* or *Devona*) is "goddess", just as the neighbouring *Dee* (< *Deva*) implies divine qualities,[33] the *Don*, like the *Dee*, was therefore, from a Pictish perspective, not just a river in which people might fish, on which they might travel by boat, which might provide water for washing and other household purposes, and so on, but at one and the same time a divine being which demanded some form of worship and adoration, perhaps even placation in times of flooding and other threats. This dual nature of certain water courses, if not all of them, may not be easily understood in our own times but may not have troubled the Pictish perception at all. If this was so, there are likely to have been particular locations on these rivers where the worship of flowing water provided special cultic significance and, in addition to the religious nature of wells and springs, these locations appear to have been at confluences. It is also possible that the divine quality of the water courses in question may have been restricted to the points where they flowed into other rivers or into the sea, especially the former, as many may not have had the same name for the whole length of their course. It may therefore have been particularly appropriate and propitious to practice "river worship" in accepted rituals, like the offering of votive objects, at confluences, elevating the ground near them to the status of *nemeton*. Confluences may thus have been regarded as "holy ground", and the term *aber* may have taken on this secondary significance in addition to its primary meaning.

This speculative thesis gains considerable support from the statistically interesting fact that at least twenty-two of the Scottish *Aber-* names once designated, or are still applied to, parishes. In those instances in which the original *Aber-* name has been replaced as a parish name (*Abercrombie* FIF, *Aberluthnot* KCD, and *Abermilk* DMF), the replacement has obvious Christian connotations (St. Monance, Marykirk and St. Mungo), bearing witness to the continued religious and cultic significance of *Aber-* places. In contrast, only three places bearing *Pit-* names (*Pitsligo* ABD, *Pittenweem* FIF, and *Pitlochry* PER) have been given parish status, and that in post-medieval times. It is highly unlikely that so many *Aber-* names were attached to parishes simply because they designated sites at confluences although this may have been a factor.

It would, of course, be rash to build this theoretical edifice on the name *Aberdeen* alone in which the river name itself bears unmistakable witness to the divine qualities of the water course. There is, however, good reason to assume that some of the other river names associated with *Aber-* sites indirectly reinforce the testimony of *Aberdeen*. The river name contained in *Arbuthnott* – *Buadhnat* – makes specific reference to the healing power of the water, the specific in the name Abernethy – * *Neithon* – praises its purity,[34] and even the river names associated with * *Aberbervie, Aberbothrie, Arbroath, Abergeldie* and *Aberargie* appear to equate actual characteristics of the flowing water with divine qualities. *Aberfeldy*, with its reference to a water-demon, and *Abertarff*, with its equation of the river with a bull-like animal, also belong to this category of names with potentially cultic significance. The latter in particular parallels names in other parts of the Celtic-speaking world, as for instance, the *Boyne* in Ireland, just as the *Dee* has several identical equivalents elsewhere. Other hydronymic specifics in *Aber-* names, as, for example, in *Aberdour*, are, of course, neutral with regard to the argument just proposed.

It is presumably no coincidence that *Aber-* names are hardly ever applied to the mouths of water courses with names which can reasonably be said to be of pre-Pictish origin; *Aberspey* and *Abertay* are late, post-Pictish names, but there are no *Aber-* sites at the mouths of the *Nairn*, the *Deveron*, the *Findhorn* and the *Earn*, whereas they are common at confluences of smaller tributaries with these and other larger rivers. The *Earn*, a major river flowing through the heart of "Pictland", for instance, has five recorded *Aber-* confluences, the Spey has three, and the Dee and the Forth have two each. There are single *Aber-* sites on the rivers Nairn, Isla, Deveron, Black Devon, Tay, the South Esk, the Don and, outside Pictland, the Annan. *Aber-* sites are also to be found on Loch Laggan, Loch Oich, and Loch Ness (two), and there are six identifiable *Aber-* names on the east coast, including the Firth of Forth. *Applecross* is the only example on the west coast and deserves special consideration, not only because of its isolated westerly location but also because of its direct reference to the cross; its Gaelic name was *a'Chomraich Abrach* "the girth or sanctuary of the *aber*", perhaps further confirmation of the second meaning of *aber* as suggested above.

The linguistic importance of *aber* as a link between Pictish and Welsh, and *p*-Celtic in general, and its toponymic status as a complementary corrective to *pet(t)* have, it is hoped, become apparent in the foregoing. It has, in the course of this discussion also become clear that it is inappropriate to consider either of these two terms, or any Pictish toponyms, separately, or to make a strong distinction between the ripuarian Picts of the *Aber-* sites and the agrarian hill-dwellers of the *Pit-* locations. A 1227 entry in the Register of Dunfermline refers to "the water that runs between the land of Petliuer and the land of Gelland on the one part and the land of Abercrumbin on the other", and it is worth remembering that "the stream at Aberlady is the Peffer".[36] Even closer links with other Pictish toponymic elements are provided by *Abergairn* ABD and, possibly, *Abercairney* PER which contain Pictish *carden* "copse, wood"; the latter also stands on a burn which joins the Peffray, thus linking three Pictish toponymic elements.

While *pett* and *aber* are undoubtedly the numerically most frequent and toponymically most substantial Pictish place name elements, it would be misleading, though tempting, to regard the recorded survival of certain other, less frequently occurring, elements as merely supportive evidence. Just as a detailed survey and intensive study of *pett-* names alone ignores the complementary information which the *aber-* names can provide concerning the life and world view of the Picts, so even the combined investigation of *pett-* and *aber-* names and of the sites they designate would still fall far short of a comprehensive investigation of all the place name material ascribable to the Picts. It cannot be the purpose of this brief essay to undertake such a full examination but reference to the existence of other Pictish toponyms and to their significance in the overall picture must nevertheless be made. Whereas the study of *pett-* names and *aber-* names has its own complexity and pitfalls, an analysis of the remaining evidence is not less complicated. In particular, the three major complicating factors already observed with regard to the *pett-* and *aber-* names also pertain to the remaining corpus: (1) Some of the names or name elements in question occur only in *pett-* name territory, i.e. in "Pictland" proper, so to speak. (2) Other names or name elements have a distribution closer to that of *aber*, i.e. are not exclusively Pictish. (3) Some Pictish toponymic elements have, like *pett*, been borrowed into Gaelic and are, in some cases, still productive parts of the Gaelic topographic vocabulary today. The toponymic components in question have had authoritative treatment by Watson, Jackson and, most recently, Fraser, and the account which follows is largely based on their findings.[37] The elements are here presented in alphabetical order.

Carden (cf. Welsh *cardden* "thicket, brake").[38] This is the specific mentioned in connection with *Abergairn* ABD and *Abercairney* PER above. It is probably best known in the compound *Kincardine*, Gaelic *Cinn-chardain*, "copse-end, wood-end", which occurs in Ross-shire, Inverness-shire (Badenoch), Perthshire (Menteith, Kincardine-on-Forth, and Blackford parish), in Kincardineshire, and in Aberdeenshire (Kincardine O'Neil). It has been suggested with considerable persuasiveness that in most of these compounds, if not in all of them, Gaelic *ceann* at an early date replaced Pictish *penn* (Welsh *pen*) "head, end", as, for instance, in Kinneil WLO (*Peanfahel* Bede) "wall-end", *Carden* is also found in such names as *Pluscarden* MOR, *Drumchardine* INV (Gaelic *druim* "ridge"), *Carden(den)* FIF, *Fettercairn* ANG (*Fothercardine, Fettercardin* Robertson's Index RMS), *Cardno* ABD (*Cardenauche* Robertson's Index, RMS), *Cairnie* ABD (*Cardenys* 1436), *Carden* ABD (*Cardene* 1512), *Card(e)ny* PER, and, on the fringe of Pictland, *Cardross* DNB (*Cardinross* 1208-33). While several Urquharts contain Gaelic *urchar* "a cast, a shot", *Urchardan* in Glen Urquhart INV (*Airchartdan* Adamnan), *Logie-Urquhart* ROS and *Urquhart* MOR are compounded with *carden*. The distribution of this toponymic element has a decidedly Pictish look (see Map III); its meaning directs us to Pictish sites near woods or at least thickets, perhaps suggesting the harvesting of

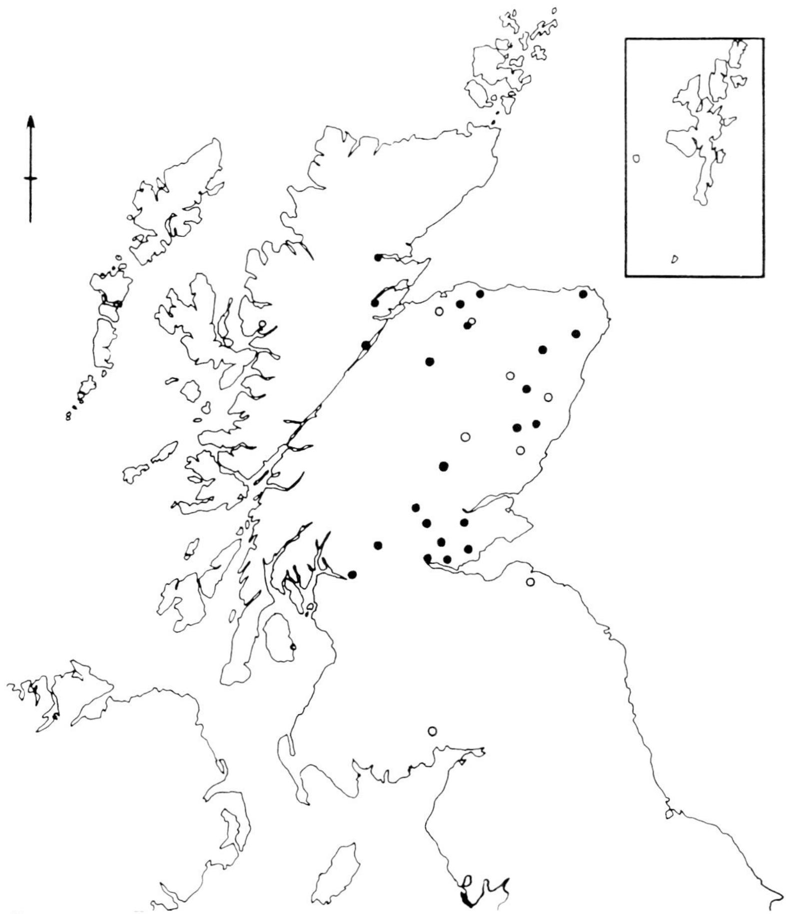

● Place names in *cardden*
○ Place names in *pres*

MAP III

timber. Names containing *carden* may in some instances have referred to natural features before becoming habitative names, a point which was discussed in connection with *aber*.

Dol (cf. Old Welsh *dol* "meadow, dole, valley") is not a very reliable indicator of Pictishness since it also survives as Gaelic *dail*, genitive *dalach*, although there is an older form *dol, doil*, genitive *dolach*.[38] Its distribution in place-name usage is therefore much wider than the area in which both *pett* and *carden* occur but it is possible that in some instances in which it is found in Pictland it may ultimately be of Pictish origin, e.g. *Dull* now Aberfeldy PER, *Chesthill*, Gaelic *Seasdul* in Glen Lyon PER, *Dulsie* NAI, *Dallas* MOR, *Dollar* CLA, and the "lost" *Abirdolo* (1580) FIF. Pictish *dol* must have been easily confused with or replaced by Gaelic *dol, dail*.

Lanerc (cf. Welsh *llanerch* "a clear space, a glade" occurs in both Pictish and Cumbric territory.[40] In the former we have two Lanricks in Perthshire and *Lendrick* in Kinross and Angus; in the latter, examples are *Lanark* LAN and Barlanark near Glasgow. Although much small in number, the distribution of *lanerc* is similar to that of *aber*.

Gaelic *monadh*, earlier *monid* "hill ground, hilly region" is a loanword from Pictish (cf. Old Breton – *monid*, Cornish *menedh*, Welsh *mynydd*).[41] Its prime example is the name of the *Mounth*; historically important was *Rigmonad*, the "royal hill" near St. Andrews FIF, the name of which survives in *Balrymonth*. Modern reflexes south of the Forth-Clyde line are *Marchmont* BWK, *Mendick* PEB, Dechmont WLO, LAN, *Montgreenan* AYR, while north of that line we have *Polmont* STL, *Moncrieff* PER, *Kinmount* PER, *Monimail* FIF, *Kininmonth* FIF, *Montquhir* ANG, *Mondynes* KCD, *Mundurno* ABD, *Essilmont* ABD, *Mountblairy* BNF, *Brightmony* NAI, *Am Monadh Liath* INV, etc. The geographical scatter of names containing *monadh* is linked with Gaelic rather than Pictish but the fact that the Pictland counties figure so prominently in the inventory of names in question is, of course, significant from the point of view of this survey.

The most easily identifiable Pictish place-name elements are, of course, those beginning with *P-* since Pictish, in contrast to Gaelic is a *p*-Celtic language. Of these, *pett* has already received close attention; other candidates are *Pan-, Par, -pawr, pefr, pen, pert, pren* and *preas*. Each one of these presents a different picture although it is probably correct to generalise by saying that wherever they occur in what used to be Pictish territory they are ultimately to be associated with the Picts.

Panbride and *Panmore* in Angus are probably the best known Scottish instances of place names containing a cognate of Welsh *pant* "valley, hollow"[42] The former is "St. Brigid's hollow", the latter corresponds to Welsh *pantmawr* "big hollow". In Angus, we also have *Panlathy* and in Aberdeenshire there is *Pannanich*. The term was, however, also used by Cumbric place-namers as names like *Pant* AYR, *Panbert Hill* ELO (1573 RMS) and *Panlaurig* BWK (1509 RMS) show. If the last of these contains – *lanrig* (*llanerch*), it would be an interesting combination of two Cumbric topographical terms which also occur in Pictland. *Panbride* in Angus has, or had, an identical equivalent in *Panbryd* AYR (1574 RMS).

Names beginning with *Par-* or *Per-* are also to be found in the whole of *p*-Celtic Scotland.[43] Watson links them with Breton *par* "a plain, a parcel of land" and Welsh *parlas* "a grassy plot". Outside Pictland there are, among others, *Pardivan* ELO, *Parduvine* MLO, *Pardovan* WLO, and *Perdovingishill* RNF (1542 RMS). There are, however, many more in Pictland itself : *Parbroath* ANG, *Pardew* FIF, *Purgavie* ANG, *Pargavie* PER, *Perwinnes* ABD, *Persey* PER, *Percie* ABD, *Pearsie* ANG, *Persie* BNF although this may rather contain *preas* "a copse" (see p. 29). This small group of names displays a distribution pattern similar to that of *pant*.

A Pictish term which has been adopted into the Gaelic topographic vocabulary is to be compared with Welsh *pawr* "pasture" and Breton *peuri* "to pasture".[44] In Gaelic it is *pór*, genitive *púir*. We have already encountered it in the name *Pitfour*; *Dalfour* BNF would be a similar all-Pictish combination. As both the generic (*dol*) and the specific (*pór*) of the latter were included into Gaelic, it is, however, uncertain whether *Dolfour* (or *Delfour* INV, MOR) was coined by Pictish or Gaelic speakers. In names like *Dochfour* INV "davach of the pasture", *Balfour* ABD, KCD, FIF (= Gaelic *Baile Phùir*), *Tillifour* ABD, *Tillyfourie* ABD "pasture hill", *Trinafour* PER (= Gaelic *Trían a'Phúir*) "third of the pasture" or *Tom a'Phúir* PER "knoll of the pasture", *pór* has been incorporated in names given by speakers of Gaelic. In fact, it is clear that *pór* was exported beyond the boundaries of Pictland since in Argyll we find *Tirafuir* (= Gaelic *Tir a'Phúir*) "land of pasture" and *Pennyfuir* (= Gaelic *Peighinn a'Phúir*) "pennyland of the pasture". Apart from these outliers, *pór*, even in its Gaelicised status, conforms pretty well to its original Pictish habitat.

Inverpeffer ANG and *Innerpeffray* PER were mentioned above as potential candidates for names in which Pictish *aber* may have been replaced by Gaelic *inbhear* (p. 17). The reason for this suggestion is that the two river names involved contain the Pictish cognate of Welsh *pefr* "radiant, beautiful".[45] The same adjective is also found in Peffery, the name of the stream which flows through *Strathpeffer*, Gaelic *Srath-pheofhair* ROSS, in the Gaelic name *Inbhir-Pheofharan*, for Dingwall which is situated at its mouth, in the *rivulus de Paforyn* (or *Peferyn*) ABD (1247), now the *Silverburn*, and in the *Paphrie Burn* ANG. Like some of the *pett-* names, it also occurs just south of the Forth in the name *Peffer Mill* on the *Braid Burn* MLO, and twice in East Lothian, one of these at Aberlady which may have been *Aberpeffer*. The term survives only in names of water courses and may, in fact, have been always associated with certain visual qualities of flowing water, in Pictish toponymic usage.

Pen "end, head" is apparently absent in Pictland but may underly some of the names now containing Gaelic *ceann*, like *Kincardine* (several), *Kinpurnie* ANG, *Kinloss* MOR, and *Kinross* KNR in which the second element is likely to be Pictish in origin.[46] Bede's *Peanfahel* (8th century) for *Kinneil* WLO demonstrates that this particular substitution did take place. *Pen* is, of course, common in Cumbric territory.

Perth PER is the most prominent example of the Pictish cognate of Welsh *perth* "bush, brake, copse" but in Angus we also find *Pert* (with Muir, Brae, and Mill of *Pert*) and the parish name *Logie Pert*, and in Stirlingshire there is *Larbert* (*Lethberth* 1195) "half-wood".[47] Records show *Perthok* and *Perteoc* in Aberdeenshire. The term appears to have been also used in Cumbric topography, as in *Pappert Hill* DNB, LAN, *Pappert Law* SLK, and possibly the *Perter Burn* DNF.

One would normally associate the toponymic usage of *pren* "tree"[48] with the Cumbric-speaking area of Scotland, i.e. the regions south of the Forth-Clyde line, as in *Pirn* PEB, MLO, *Pirnie* and *Primside* ROX, *Barnbougle* WLO, *Traprain* ELO, and so on. The two names *Primrose* in Berwickshire and Midlothian do, however, have an identical equivalent in Fife; all of them are derived from *pren ros* "tree of the moor", just as *Prinlaws* FIF is *Pren las* "green tree'. In Pictland, *pren* has also found reflexes in *Pairney* PER and *Kinpurnie* ANG, the latter a potential candidate for an earlier **Pen-purnie*.

A term which has been borrowed into Gaelic is *pres*, now Gaelic *preas* "thicket";[49] this is cognate with Welsh *prys* "covert". There can be no doubt that names like *Preas Braigh nan Allt* SUT, *Preas an Uisge* ROS, and *Preas nan Seanachar* ROS must have been given by Gaelic speakers, and the name *Dumfries* DMF may have its origins in a Cumbric-Gaelic environment, but there are also several examples of *pres/preas* in Pictland; *Presmuckerach* in Badenoch INV, *Prescalton* and *Pressley* MOR, *Preshome* BNF, *Prescoly* ABD (1390 RMS), *Presquheill* ABD (1577 RMS), *Terpersie* ABD (*Tirepressy* 1391), *Dalpersie* ABD, *Culperso* KCD, *Presnerb* PER, *Pressock* PER (1529 RMS), *Pressmuk* PER (1511 RMS), *Bofressely* PER (1480 RMS).

Naturally, all these place-name elements deserve much closer scrutiny but that is beyond the scope of this essay. Nor can it be claimed that the names paraded form the whole of the corpus of types and elements ascribable to a Pictish place-nomenclature; several of the terms designated as British or British-Gaelic by Watson may well, in addition to the ones already discussed, have a Pictish dimension. What is significant, however, is the observation that all these elements did not primarily refer to a place of human habitation but to natural features in the landscape. Especially noteworthy is the fact that so many of them make reference to woodlands, whether as places of work or, on their edges, as settlement sites. In Fraser's felicitous summing up of the situation, they "suggest that the Caledonia Silva was a potent factor in the distribution of settlement and that it laid considerable constraints on human activity."[50] As a group they point to a third topographical component in the lives of the Picts – the woods – thus complementing the evidence provided by *pett* and *aber*.

In contrast, the Cumbric place-nomenclature contains a number of elements primarily related to human habitation, particularly *caer* (*Carluke, Castairs, Carlisle*) and *tref* (*Traprain, Tranent, Traquair*) but the former is not unknown in Pictland (*Carpow, Cargill, Cardeen* PER; *Kirkbuddo*, formerly *Kerbuddo*, ANG; and, of course, *Kirkcaldy* [*Kircalathin* 1150] and *Crail* [*Caraile* 1150-52] in Fife) and the type of name in which *tref* appears as a second element in combination with a Gaelic first element (*Capledrae* FIF, *Clinterly* ABD, *Fintry* STL, ABD, *Fintray* ABD, *Fortree, Fortrie, Fortry* ABD, BNF) still has to be evaluated systematically, especially in comparison with the corresponding evidence in Cumbric territory, sometimes producing identical doublets, as in *Trostrie* KCB and *Troustrie* FIF, or *Rattra* KCB and *Rattray* PER, ABD.[51] Recent discussions of such elements as *both*[52] and *lios* are also relevant here. It would therefore be far too simplistic to say that all Pictish place names primarily refer to natural features, even though many of them, of course, do.

As a coda, a comment on the mobility acquired by certain Pictish place names since the time when Scottish surnames became heritable is perhaps not out of place.[53] As is well known, one of the four sources of surnames in our culture are the names of places from which people have moved thus making them outsiders or strangers in their new communities. This transfer of items from one onomastic category – names of places – to another – names of persons –, in itself quite a fascinating phenomenon, allows us sometimes to ascertain to places of origin of people and their degree of mobility. Some of the Pictish place names which have become surnames in this process are *Abercorn, Abercrombie, Aberdeen, Aberdour, Abernethy, Arbuthnott, Pitbladdo, Pitcairn, Pitcaithly, Pittendreich*, and *Pittilock/Pittilloch* (cf. *Pittillo, Patullo*, etc.). Without going into any detail, it is interesting to note that whereas some of these names, together with their bearers, of course, have moved quite far afield, whereas others have more or less stayed in Pictland. Some of them have produced large numbers of bearers whereas others have applied to only a few families. Worth noting, too, is the magnetic power with which cities like Edinburgh and Glasgow attracted bearers of Pictish locative surnames, while their presence in the Highlands is confined to a few individuals. The cultural border appears to have been very strong in that respect.

The study of Pictish place names in Scotland has made great strides forward in the last few decades. There is, however, much that can be and has to be still explored to realise the full potential of the place names of Pictland as rich sources of information about the language, lives, and world-view of the Picts.

NOTES AND REFERENCES

[1] See, for example, Stevenson 1955: 100, 105, 124; Henderson 1967: 109 and 111; Henderson 1975: 114-115; A. Jackson 1984: 93-95.

[2] See, for instance, K.H. Jackson 1955: 146, 150; Nicolaisen 1975: 106-107; Nicolaisen 1976a: 153, 163; I.A. Fraser 1987: 69; Nicolaisen 1995: 12.

[3] Note the similarities between the distribution of the Class II symbol stones and that of the place names containing *pett* (Nicolaisen 1976a: 153, 155).

[4] See for a recent view Forsyth 1995: 7-10.

[5] "Cumbric" is the term which was first suggested by K.H. Jackson (see 1963: 63) for the *p*-Celtic language once spoken south of the Forth-Clyde line.

[6] W.F. Skene (1836: 67-76) was of the opinion that the Picts were Goidels; his views are discussed by Alexander Macbain (1896-97: 191-214). The equation of Gaelic and Pictish was continued by Diack (1926: 83-98; 1944) and, less radically, by J. Fraser (1927).

[7] K.H. Jackson suggested that, archaeologically speaking, Pictish may have had Hallstatt antecedents whereas Cumbric (Brittonic) was primarily the *p*-Celtic dialect of La Tene (1955: 156).

[8] As late as 1906, however, W.C. Mackenzie was able to claim "the impossibility, in the present state of our knowledge, of classifying with any certainty the mysterious Picts, either with the Celtic or with the Teutonic elements of which the Scottish nation is mainly composed … The language of the Picts continues to be a sealed book" (1906: 172).

[9] See Forsyth 1995: 9.

[10] The main proponent of this theory is K.H. Jackson (1955: 152), whose views have influence those of many scholars including my own.

[11] This was a view held by John Rhŷs (1891-92 and 1892-93). While relating Pictish to Basque in this article, Rhŷs later abandons this opinion (1897-98). Non-Indo-European origin of the Picts was also proposed by Zimmer (1898), E. MacNeill (1933 and 1939) and Macalister (1940).

[12] Sverdrup 1995.

[13] Nicolaisen 1957, 1971, 1982a and b, 1991, with a summary in Nicolaisen 1976a: 179-91; but see also Jackson 1955: 132.

[14] An excellent overview of the questions and theories proposed and, particularly, of the evidence is Marjorie O. Anderson's discussion of "Picts – the Name and the People" (1987). Of earlier accounts see

especially Wainwright 1955 and Chadwick 1958.

15 See Nicolaisen 1976a; 150-51.

16 Rivet and Smith 1979: 438-440; see also Nicolaisen 1956b: 138.

17 Jackson (1955: 148), however, considers the possibility of links with Gaulish.

18 That Pictish was a *p*-Celtic language is now the accepted doctrine, and there is no reason to question that linguistic ascription for the purposes of this essay. Strong support for it has come from Stokes (1890: 392), MacBain 1892, MacBain 1897: 211, Watson 1904-05, Watson 1921, Watson 1926: 70-72, 126-27, O'Rahilly 1946: 353-84, 529-38, K.H. Jackson 1955: 132, Nicolaisen 1972; Nicolaisen 1976a: 154, Nicolaisen 1976b: 125-26, Nicolaisen 1995a and b.

19 See Watson 1926: 407-14; J. Fraser 1942; K.H. Jackson 1955: 146-48; Nicolaisen 1976a: 151-58; Nicolaisen 1995a.

20 K.H. Jackson 1972: 19-20.

21 See I.A. Fraser 1986.

22 Whittington and Soulsby 1968: 117. See also Whittington 1974-75.

23 Nicolaisen 1996.

24 Taylor 1995: 64.

25 Taylor, personal communication. See also Taylor 1994; 1995: 61. K.H. Jackson was more cautious when attempting an English translation of *pett*, noting that it is almost impossible to translate it with one single word. He favoured "estate" or "parcel of land" but also suggested that "it probably meant … not merely a unit of land but a unit of population", not unlike the mediaeval "manor" (K.H. Jackson 1972: 114).

26 The following lists are largely based on Watson 1926: 408-14.

27 See Watson 1926: 407.

28 Taylor 1995: 61.

29 Watson 1926: 458-67; K.H. Jackson 1955: 148-49; Nicolaisen 1976a: 164-65. The now thoroughly refuted view that *aber* is to be equated with Gaelic was held by Diack (1926: 83-98; 1944: 126-34) and J. Fraser (1927: 192-4).

30 This inventory mostly based on Watson 1926: 458-67, also forms the illustrative material of an article of mine "On Pictish Rivers and their Confluences" in a forthcoming volume entitled *The Worm, the Germ and the Thorn*. It is here included with the editor's kind permission.

31 See note 13 above.

32 Diack, in his harsh review of Erskine Beveridge's *The Abers and Invers of Scotland* (Diack 1926), is particularly adamant on this subject. In spite of his criticism, Beveridge's book (Beveridge 1923) is still a handy

source for information about the names in question and their early spellings.

[33] See Nicolaisen 1990: 59-62; also Nicolaisen (in press). See further Rivet and Smith 1979: 336-38.

[34] The Gaulish god **Nectonos* functioned specifically as the god of hot springs and healing.

[35] See Nicolaisen (in press).

[36] Watson 1926: 461.

[37] Watson 1926: chapters XI and XII; K.H. Jackson 1955: 148-49; I.A. Fraser 1987; see also Nicolaisen 1975a: 169-70.

[38] Watson 1926: 352-53; I.A. Fraser 1987: 70.

[39] *Ibid.* : 414-19; I.A. Fraser 1987: 68.

[40] *Ibid.* : 356.

[41] *Ibid.* : 391-407.

[42] *Ibid.* : 373-74.

[43] *Ibid.* : 372-73.

[44] *Ibid.* : 376-77.

[45] *Ibid.* : 452-53.

[46] *Ibid.* : 353-56.

[47] *Ibid.* : 356-57.

[48] *Ibid.* : 351-52.

[49] *Ibid.* : 419-22; I.A. Fraser 1987: 69-70.

[50] I.A. Fraser 1987: 69. This statement is true regardless of what the "Caledonian Forest" actually looked like on the ground.

[51] Watson 1926: 357-67; Nicolaisen 1976a: 167: 70.

[52] Taylor 1996: 95-98.

[53] Nicolaisen 1991-92.

BIBLIOGRAPHY

Anderson, Marjorie O. 1987. "Picts – the Name and the People". In: Small 1987: 7-14.

Beveridge, Erskine. 1923. *The 'Abers' and 'Invers' of Scotland*. Edinburgh.

Chadwick, Nora K. 1958. "The Name Pict". *Scottish Gaelic Studies* 8: 146-76.

Diack, Francis C. 1926. "Aber and Inver in Scotland". *Scottish Gaelic Studies* 1: 83-98.

– 1944. *The Inscriptions of Pictland*, Aberdeen, Third Spalding Club.

Forsyth, Katherine. 1995. "Language in Pictland, spoken and written". In: Nicoll 1995: 7-10.

Fraser, I.A. 1986. "Norse and Celtic Place-Names around the Dornoch Firth". In: John R. Baldwin (ed.), *Firthlands of Ross and Sutherland*, Edinburgh, Scottish Society for Northern Studies, 23-32.

– 1987. "The Picts – A New Look at Old Problems". In: Small 1987: 68-72.

Fraser, J. 1927. "The Question of the Picts". *Scottish Gaelic Studies* 2: 172-201.

– 1942. "Pet(t) in Place Names". *Scottish Gaelic Studies* 5: 67-71.

Henderson, Isabel. 1967. *The Picts*. London.

– 1975. Maps in: McNeill and Nicholson 1975: 114-15.

Jackson, Anthony. 1984. *The Symbol Stones of Scotland*. Stromness, Orkney.

Jackson. K.H. 1955. "The Pictish Language". In: Wainwright 1955, 129-66.

– 1963. "Angles and Britons in Northumbria and Cumbria". In: *Angles and Britons*. Cardiff, 60-84.

– 1972. *The Gaelic Notes in the Book of Deer*. Cambridge.

Macalister, R.A.S. 1940. "The Inscription and Language of the Picts". In: John Ryan (ed.), *Essays and Studies presented to Professor Eoin MacNeill*. Dublin, 184-226.

Macbain, A. 1892. "Ptolemy's Geography of Scotland". *Transactions of the Gaelic Society of Inverness* 18: 267-88.

– 1896-97. "Mr Skene versus Dr Skene". *Transactions of the Gaelic Society of Inverness* 21: 191-214.

Mackenzie, W.C. 1906. "Picts and Pets". *The Antiquary*; 172-75.

MacNeill, E. 1933. "The Pretanic Background in Britain and Ireland". *The Journal of the Royal Society of Antiquaries in Ireland* 63: 1-28.

– 1939. "The Language of the Picts". *Yorkshire Celtic Studies* 2: 3-45.
MacNeill, Peter, and Nicholson, Ranald. *An Historical Atlas of Scotland* c. 400-c.1600. St. Andrews.
Nicolaisen, W.F.H. 1957. "Die alteuropäischen Gewässernamen der britischen Hauptinsel". *Beiträge zur Namenforschung* 8: 211-68.
– 1972. "*P*-Celtic Place-Names in Scotland: A Reappraisal". *Studia Celtica* 7: 1-11.
– 1975. Maps in MacNeill and Nicholson, 1975: 106-07.
– 1976a. *Scottish Place-Names: Their Study and Significance*. London.
– 1976b. "Celtic Toponymics in Scotland". *Word* 28: 117-39.
– 1982a. "Thirty Years Later: Thoughts on a Viable Concept of an Old European Hydronymy". In: Winkelman, Otto and Braisch, Maria (eds.), *Festschrift für Johannes Hubschmid zum 65. Geburtstag*. Bern, 139-48.
– 1982b. " 'Old European' Names in Britain". *Nomina* 6: 3742.
– 1990. "Aberdeen: A Toponymic Key to the Region". *Northern studies* 27: 50-63.
– 1991. "Die ältesten Namenschichten auf den Britischen Inseln". *Beiträge zur Namenforschung*, N.F., Beiheft 32. Heidelberg, 67-74.
– 1991-92. "Pictish Place-Names as Scottish Surnames. Origins, Dissemination and Current Status". *Nomina* 15: 7-20.
– 1995a. "Pictish Place Names". In Nicoll 1995: 11-13.
– 1995b. "Something Old, Something New from the Lands of the Picts". In: Michaela Ofitsch and Christian Zinko (eds.), *Studia Onomastica et Indogermanica*. Arbeiten aus der Abteilung 'Vergleichende Sprachwissenschaft' Graz 10: 137-42.
– 1996. "Search for Pittendreich". *Leopard* (January 1996): 25.
– (in press). "The *Dee* at Chester and Aberdeen: Thoughts on Rivers and Divinities". In: Alex Rumble *et al.* (eds.), *Memorial Volume for John McN. Dodgson*.
Nicoll, Eric H. 1995. *A Pictish Panorama*. Balgavies, Angus.
O'Rahilly, T.F. 1946. *Early Irish History and Mythology*. Dublin.
Rhŷs, John. 1891-92. "The Inscriptions and Language of the Northern Picts". *Proceedings of the Society of Antiquaries of Scotland* 26: 263-351.
– 1892-93. "Addenda et Corrigenda". *Ibid*. 27: 411-12.
– 1897-98. "A Revised Account of the Northern Picts". *Ibid*. 32: 324-98.
Rivet, A.L.F., and Smith, Colin. 1979. *The Place-Names of Roman Britain*. Princeton, N.S.

Skene, W.F. 1836. *The Highlanders of Sutherland*. London.

Small, Alan (ed.) 1987. *The Picts: A New Look at Old Problems*. Dundee.

Stevenson, Robert B.K. 1955. "Pictish Art". In: Wainwright 1955: 97-128.

Stokes, W. 1890. "On the Linguistic Value of the Irish Annals." *Transactions of the Philological Society* (1888-90): 365-433.

Sverdrup, Harald U. 1995. *Classifying and translating inscriptions in the Pictish language*. Reports in ecology and environmental engineering 4. Lund (Sweden).

Taylor, Simon. 1994. "Some Early Scottish Place Names and Queen Margaret". *Scottish Language* 13: 1-17.

– 1995. *Settlement-names in Fife*. Unpublished PhD Thesis. University of Edinburgh.

– 1996. "Place-names and the Early Church in Scotland". In: Crawford, Barbara E. (Ed.), *Scotland in Dark Age Britain*. St. Andrews, 93-110.

Wainwright, F.T. (ed.), 1955. *The Problem of the Picts*. Edinburgh.

Watson, W.J. 1905-05. "The Study of Highland Place-Names". *The Celtic Review* 1: 22-31.

– 1921. *The Picts: Their Original Position in Scotland*. Inverness. Also in: *Transactions of the Gaelic Society of Inverness*. 30 (1919-22): 240-61.

– 1926. *The History of the Celtic Place-Names of Scotland*. Edinburgh.

Whittington, G. 1975. "Placenames and the settlement pattern of dark-age Scotland". *Proceedings of the Society of Antiquaries of Scotland* 106 (1974-75): 99-110.

Whittington, G. and Soulsby, A.J. 1968. "A Preliminary Report on an Investigation into Pit Place-Names". *Scottish Geographical Magazine* 84: 117-25.

Zimmer, H. 1898. "Matriarchy among the Picts". In: Henderson, G., *Leabhar nan Gleann*. Edinburgh 1898, 1-42.

COUNTY ABBREVIATIONS

ABD	Aberdeenshire
ANG	Angus
AYR	Ayrshire
BNF	Banffshire
BTE	Bute
BWK	Berwickshire
CAI	Caithness
CLA	Clackmananshire
DMF	Drumfriesshire
DNB	Dumbartonshire
ELO	East Lothian
FIF	Fife
INV	Inverness-shire
KCB	Kirkcudbrightshire
KCD	Kincardineshire
KNR	Kinross-shire
LAN	Lanarkshire
MLO	Midlothian
MOR	Morayshire
NAI	Nairnshire
ORK	Orkney
PEB	Peebles-shire
PER	Perthshire
RNF	Renfrewshire
ROS	Ross and Cromarty
ROX	Roxburghshire
SHE	Shetland
SLK	Selkirkshire
STL	Stirlingshire
SUT	Sutherland
WIG	Wigtonshire
WLO	West Lothian

The county designations are those used before the administrative restructuring in the early 1970s.

SOURCE ABBREVIATION

RMS Resistrum Magni Sigilli Regum Scotorum
= Register of the Great Seal. Edinburgh